SOMETHING *more* FOR THE GIRLS

Arranged by DAN COATES
for easy piano

D1567625

Project Manager: CAROL CUELLAR
Art Design: CARMEN FORTUNATO
DAN COATES® is a registered trademark of Warner Bros. Publications.

© 2001 WARNER BROS. PUBLICATIONS
All Rights Reserved

CONTENTS

CAN'T FIGHT THE MOONLIGHT
(FROM "COYOTE UGLY") . . . . . LeAnn Rimes 4

COLORS OF THE WIND . . . . Vanessa Williams 8

GRADUATION
(FRIENDS FOREVER) . . . . Vitamin C 24

I HOPE YOU DANCE . . . . Lee Ann Womack 12

I STILL BELIEVE . . . . Mariah Carey 16

I THINK I'M IN LOVE WITH YOU . .Jessica Simpson 20

I TURN TO YOU . . . . Christina Aguilera 29

I'M YOUR ANGEL . . . . R. Kelly & Celine Dion 34

THE LITTLE GIRL . . . . John Michael Montgomery 39

LUCKY . . . . Britney Spears 42

MY EVERYTHING . . . . 98° 46

OOPS!...I DID IT AGAIN . . . . Britney Spears 54

SHAPE OF MY HEART . . . . Backstreet Boys 50

SHOW ME THE MEANING
OF BEING LONELY . . . . Backstreet Boys 59

SOMETIMES . . . . Britney Spears 64

SOMEWHERE OUT THERE . . . . . .James Ingram & Linda Ronstadt .80

STRONGER . . . . Britney Spears 68

THAT'S THE WAY IT IS . . . . Celine Dion 72

THIS I PROMISE YOU . . . . *NSYNC 76

TO LOVE YOU MORE . . . . Celine Dion 83

A WHOLE NEW WORLD . . . . Peabo Bryson & Regina Belle . . .88

Dan Coates

As a student at the University of Miami, Dan Coates paid his tuition by playing the piano at south Florida nightclubs and restaurants. One evening in 1975, after Dan had worked his unique brand of magic on the ivories, a stranger from the music field walked up and told him that he should put his inspired piano arrangements down on paper so they could be published.

Dan took the stranger's advice—and the world of music has become much richer as a result. Since that chance encounter long ago, Dan has gone on to achieve international acclaim for his brilliant piano arrangements. His Big Note, Easy Piano and Professional Touch arrangements have inspired countless piano students and established themselves as classics against which all other works must be measured.

Enjoying an exclusive association with Warner Bros. Publications since 1982, Dan has demonstrated a unique gift for writing arrangements intended for students of every level, from beginner to advanced. Dan never fails to bring a fresh and original approach to his work. Pushing his own creative boundaries with each new manuscript, he writes material that is musically exciting and educationally sound.

From the very beginning of his musical life, Dan has always been eager to seek new challenges. As a five-year-old in Syracuse, New York, he used to sneak into the home of his neighbors to play their piano. Blessed with an amazing ear for music, Dan was able to imitate the melodies of songs he had heard on the radio. Finally, his neighbors convinced his parents to buy Dan his own piano. At that point, there was no stopping his musical development. Dan won a prestigious New York State competition for music composers at the age of 15. Then, after graduating from high school, he toured the world as an arranger and pianist with the group Up With People.

Later, Dan studied piano at the University of Miami with the legendary Ivan Davis, developing his natural abilities to stylize music on the keyboard. Continuing to perform professionally during and after his college years, Dan has played the piano on national television and at the 1984 Summer Olympics in Los Angeles. He has also accompanied recording artists as diverse as Dusty Springfield and Charlotte Rae.

During his long and prolific association with Warner Bros. Publications, Dan has written many awardwinning books. He conducts piano workshops worldwide, demonstrating his famous arrangements with a special spark that never fails to inspire students and teachers alike.

CAN'T FIGHT THE MOONLIGHT
(Theme from Coyote Ugly)

Words and Music by
DIANE WARREN
Arranged by DAN COATES

Moderate, steady beat (♩ = 98)

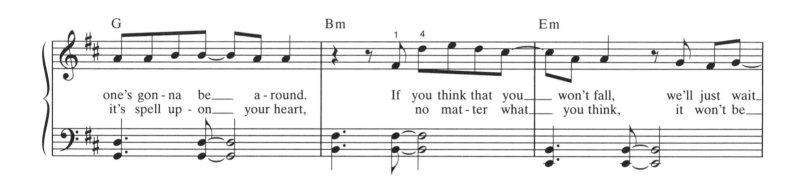

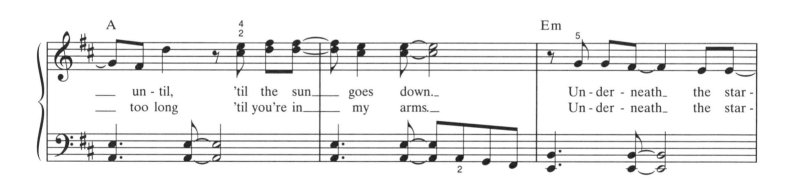

Can't Fight the Moonlight - 4 - 1

Chorus:

It will take_ you in_ to-night.
Feel it steal_ your heart_ to-night. } You can try_ to re - sist,_ try to hide_

_ from my kiss,_ but you know,_ but you know_ that you can't fight the moon - light. Deep_

_ in the dark,_ you'll sur - ren - der your heart._ Don't you know,_ don't you know_ that you

can't fight the moon - light, no, you can't fight_ it. It's

gon - na get to your heart. no, you can't fight_ it._

6

No mat-ter what___ you do, the night is gon-na get to you.

Bridge:

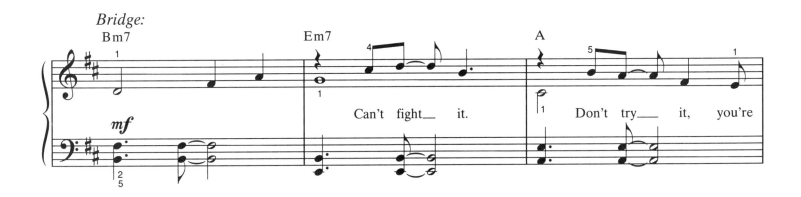

Can't fight___ it. Don't try___ it, you're

nev-er gon-na win, 'cause un-der-neath___ the star - light, star - light,___

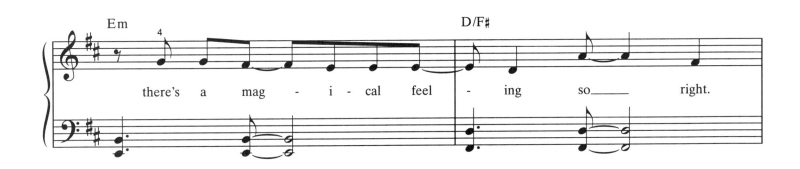

there's a mag - i - cal feel - ing so_____ right.

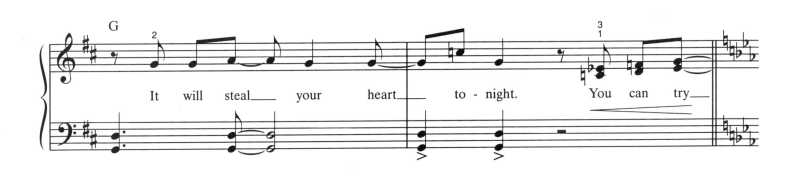

It will steal___ your heart___ to - night. You can try___

Chorus:

to re-sist,_ try to hide_ from my kiss,_ but you know,_ but you know_ that you

can't fight the moon-light. Deep_ in the dark,_ you'll sur-ren - der your heart._ Don't you know,_

_ don't you know_ that you can't fight the moon - light, no, you can't fight_

_ it. You can try_ _ it. It's gon-na get to your heart._

COLORS OF THE WIND

Lyrics by
STEPHEN SCHWARTZ

Music by
ALAN MENKEN
Arranged by DAN COATES

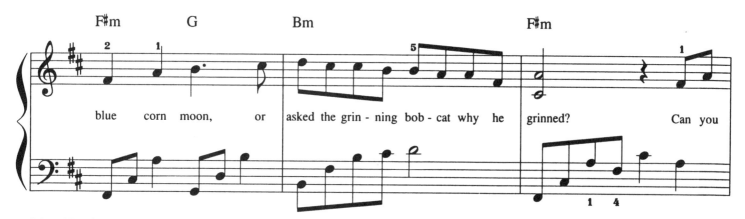

Colors of the Wind - 4 - 4

I HOPE YOU DANCE

Words and Music by
MARK D. SANDERS and TIA SILLERS
Arranged by DAN COATES

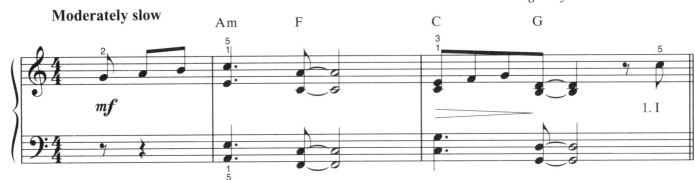

Verse:

hope you nev - er lose your sense of won - der. You get your
2. *See additional lyrics*

fill to eat, but al - ways keep that hun - ger. May you

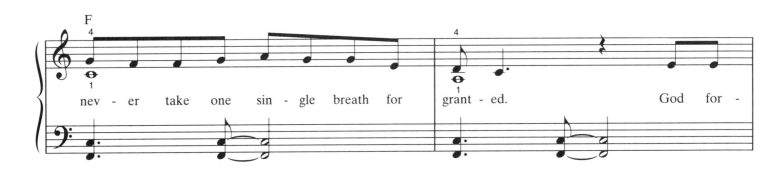

nev - er take one sin - gle breath for grant - ed. God for -

I Hope You Dance - 4 - 1

14

Verse 2:
I hope you never fear those mountains in the distance,
Never settle for the path of least resistance.
Livin' might mean takin' chances but they're worth takin'.
Lovin' might be a mistake but it's worth makin'.
(To Chorus 2:)

Chorus 2:
Don't let some hell-bent heart leave you bitter.
When you come close to sellin' out, reconsider.
Give the heavens above more than just a passing glance.
And when you get the choice to sit it out or dance,
I hope you dance.
(Repeat Chorus 1:)

I STILL BELIEVE

Words and Music by
ANTONINA ARMATO and
BEPPE CANTORELLI
Arranged by DAN COATES

I Still Believe - 4 - 1

18

I THINK I'M IN LOVE WITH YOU

Words and Music by
MARK ROONEY, DAN SHEA
and JOHN MELLENCAMP
Arranged by DAN COATES

Bright dance tempo (♩ = 106)

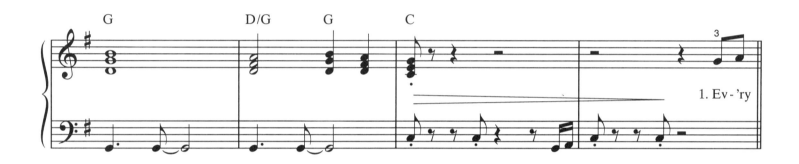

Verse:

time your near, ba-by,   I get kind of cra-zy in my   head for you___ and I don't know

2. *See additional lyrics*

what to do.___   And oh, ba-by,   I get kind of shak-y when they

I Think I'm in Love With You - 4 - 1

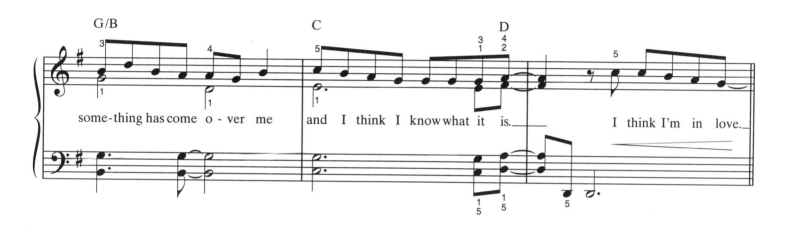

Chorus:

tell - in' all my friends what I feel for you.___ 2. Just the

1.

feel for you.___

2.

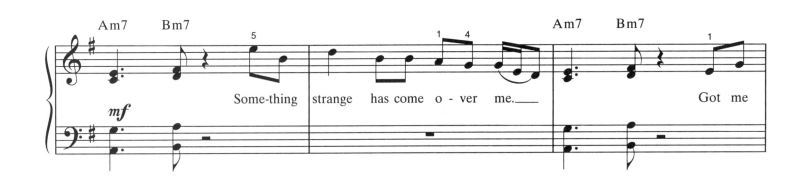

Some-thing strange has come o - ver me.___

Got me

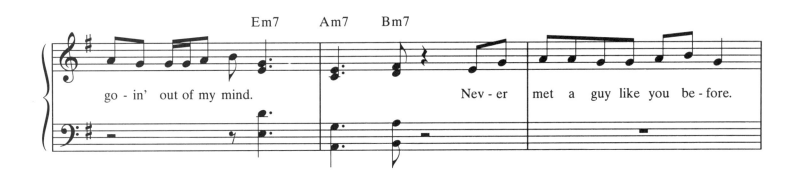

go - in' out of my mind.

Nev - er met a guy like you be - fore.

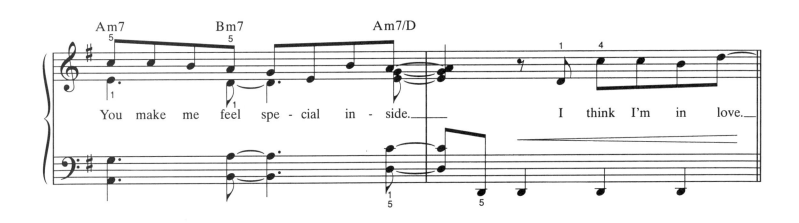

You make me feel spe - cial in - side.___

I think I'm in love.___

Boy, I think that I'm in love with you.___ Got me do-in' sil-ly things_ when it

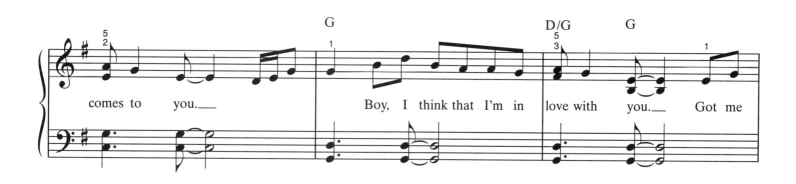

comes to you.___ Boy, I think that I'm in love with you.___ Got me

tell-in' all my friends_ what I feel for you.___ I'm in love.___

Verse 2:
Just the other night, baby,
I saw you hangin'.
You were with your crew.
I was with mine, too.
You took me by surprise
When you turned and looked me
In my eyes.
Oh, you really blew my mind.
I don't know what's gotten into me,
But I kinda think I know what it is.
I think I'm in love.
(To Chorus:)

GRADUATION
(Friends Forever)

Words and Music by
COLLEEN FITZPATRICK
and JOSH DEUTSCH
Arranged by DAN COATES

Moderately slow (♩ = 160)

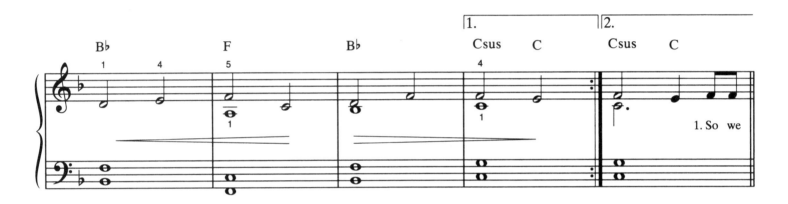

Verse:

talked all night a - bout the rest of our lives,___ where we're gon - na be when we turn___

___ twen - ty - five.___ I keep think - ing times will nev - er change,___

Graduation - 5 - 1

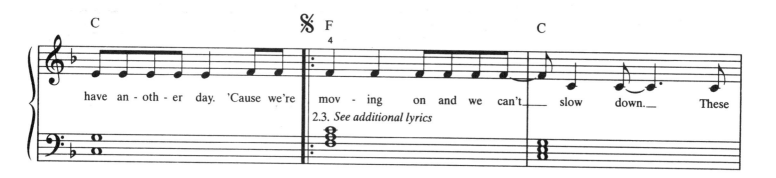

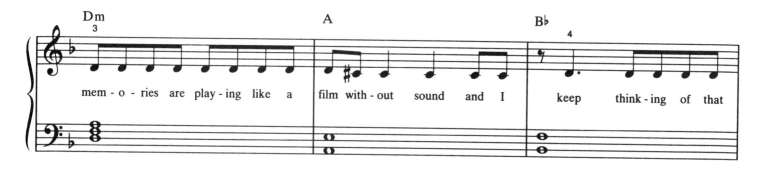

Graduation - 5 - 2

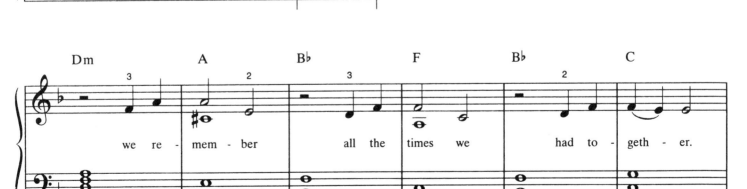

come what - ev - er,   we will still be   friends for - ev - er.

Verse 2:
So if we get the big jobs and we make the big money,
When we look back at now, will our jokes still be funny?
Will we still remember everything we learned in school,
Still be trying to break every single rule?
Will little brainy Bobby be the stockbroker man?
Can Heather find a job that won't interfere with her tan?
I keep thinking that it's not goodbye,
Keep on thinking it's our time to fly.
(To Chorus:)

Verse 3:
Will we think about tomorrow like we think about now?
Can we survive it out there, can we make it somehow?
I guess I thought that this would never end,
And suddenly it's like we're women and men.
Will the past be a shadow that will follow us around?
Will the memories fade when I leave this town?
I keep thinking that it's not goodbye,
Keep thinking it's our time to fly.
(To Chorus:)

I TURN TO YOU

Words and Music by
DIANE WARREN
Arranged by DAN COATES

Slowly (♩=76)

I Turn to You - 5 - 1

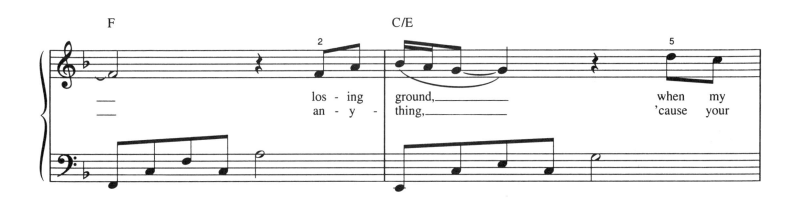

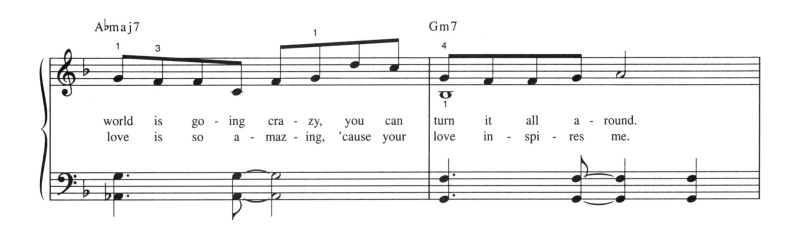

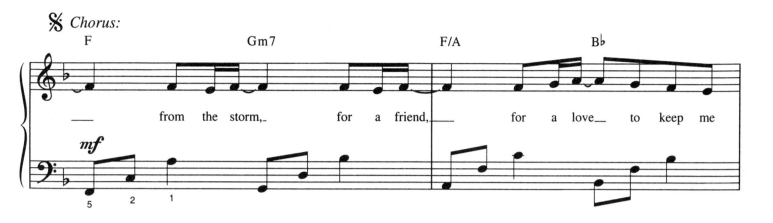

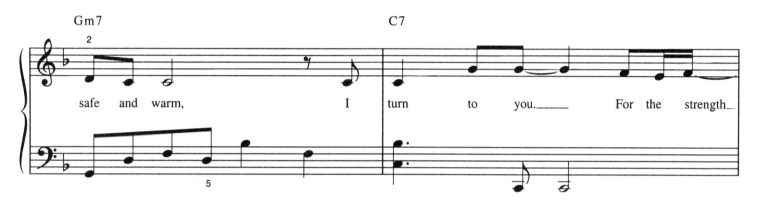

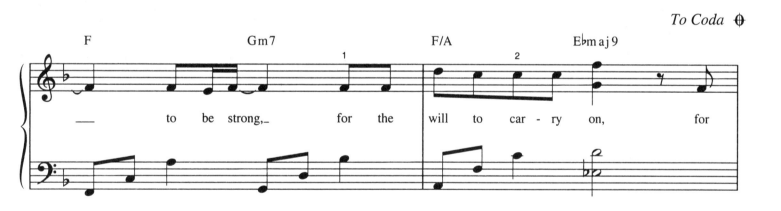

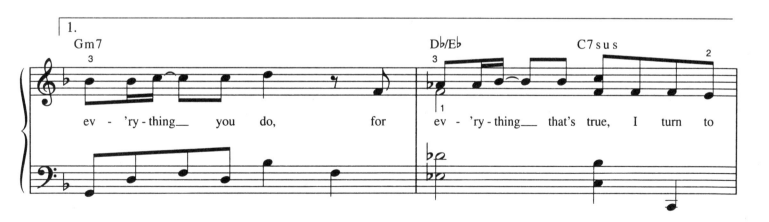

32

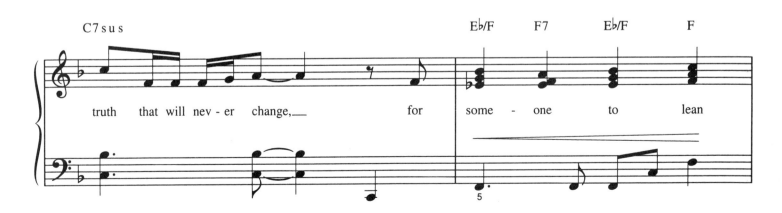

I Turn to You - 5 - 4

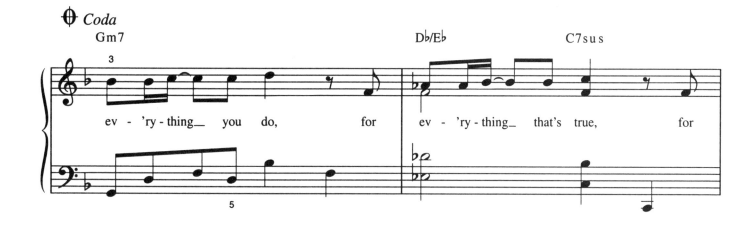

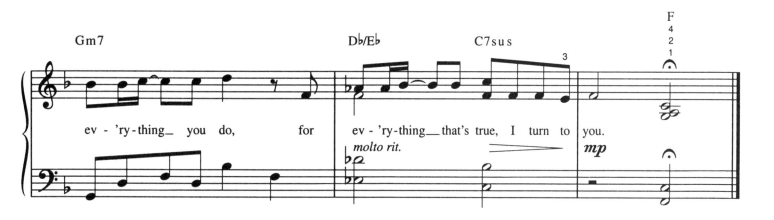

I'M YOUR ANGEL

Words and Music by
R. KELLY
Arranged by DAN COATES

I'm Your Angel - 5 - 1

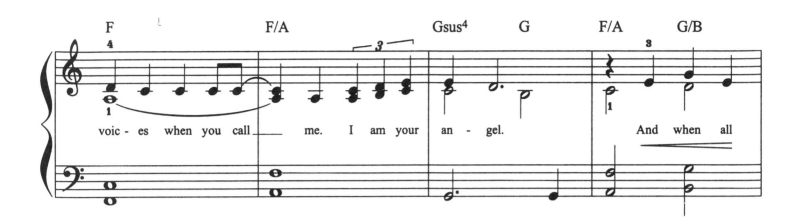

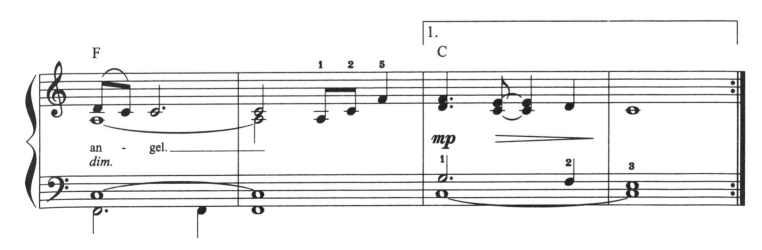

38

THE LITTLE GIRL

Words and Music by
HARLEY ALLEN
Arranged by DAN COATES

Moderately slow ballad (♩= 88)

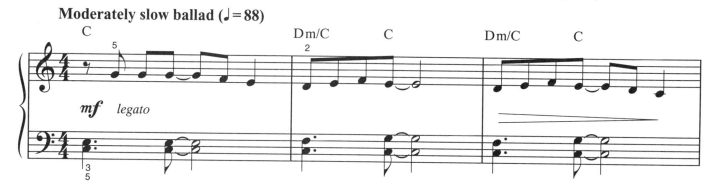

Verse 1:

1. Her par - ents nev - er took the young girl to church,_ nev - er

spoke of His name,_ nev - er read her His word._ Two non - be - liev - ers walk - ing

lost in this world,_ took their ba - by with them._ What a sad lit - tle girl._

The Little Girl - 3 - 1

Oh, what a sad lit-tle life.

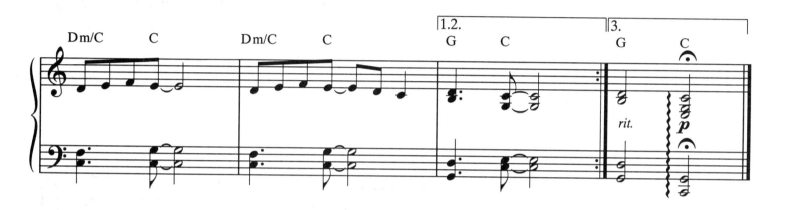

Verse 3:
And like it always does, the bad just got worse,
With every slap and every curse.
Until her daddy, in a drunk rage one night,
Used a gun on her mom and then took his life.

Chorus 2:
And some people from the city
Took the girl far away
To a new mom and a new dad,
Kisses and hugs every day.

Verse 4:
Her first day of Sunday school, the teacher walked in,
And a small little girl stared at a picture of Him.
She said, "I know that man up there on that cross.
I don't know his name, but I know he got off."

Chorus 3:
"'Cause He was there in my old house
And held me close to His side
As I hid there behind our couch
The night that my parents died."

The Little Girl - 3 - 3

LUCKY

Words and Music by
MAX MARTIN, RAMI
and ALEXANDER KRONLUND
Arranged by DAN COATES

Moderate, steady beat (♩ = 96)

Verse 1:

1. Ear - ly morn-ing, she wakes up. Knock, knock, knock on the door.

It's time for make-up, per-fect smile. It's you they're all wait-ing for. They go,

Chorus:

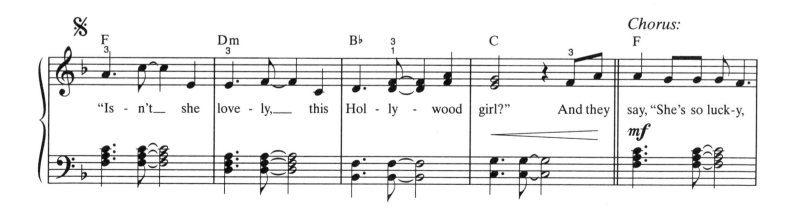

"Is - n't__ she love - ly,__ this Hol - ly - wood girl?" And they say, "She's so luck-y,

44

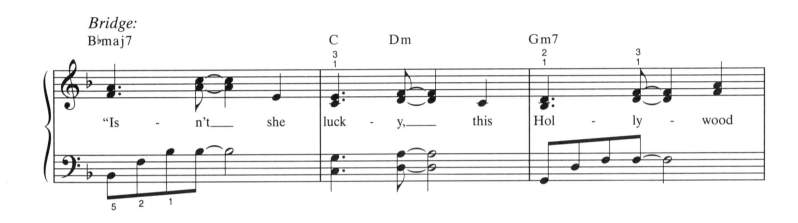

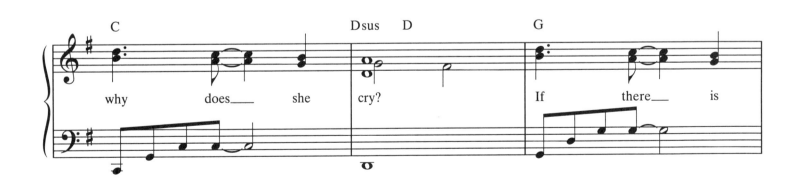

Lucky - 4 - 3

noth - ing___ miss - ing in her life, why do tears come___ at night?

Chorus:

mf "She's so luck - y, she's a star." But she cry, cry, cries in her

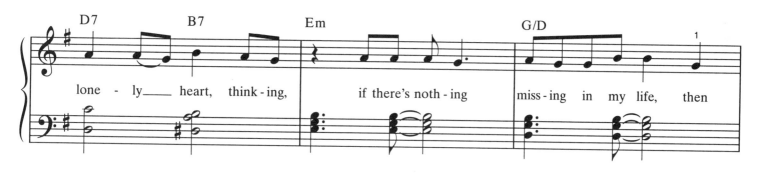

lone - ly___ heart, think - ing, if there's noth - ing miss - ing in my life, then

why do___ these tears come___ at night? tears come___ at night?

MY EVERYTHING

Words and Music by
ARNTHOR BIRGISSON, ANDERS SVEN BAGGE,
NICK LACHEY and ANDREW LACHEY
Arranged by DAN COATES

Slowly, with expression
Verse:

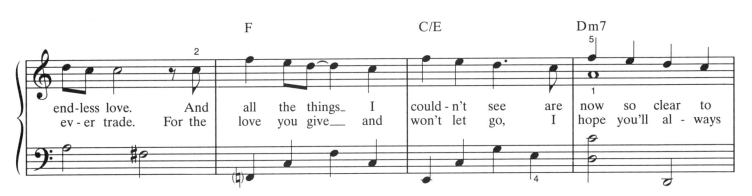

My Everything - 4 - 1

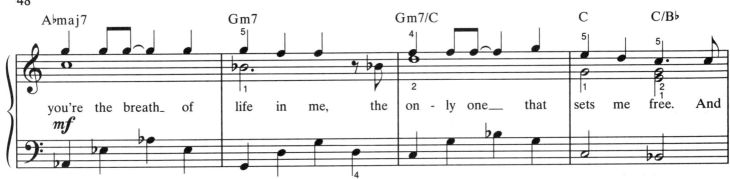

you're the breath of life in me, the on - ly one that sets me free. And

you have made my soul com - plete for all time. You are my

ev - 'ry-thing. Noth - ing your love won't bring. My life is

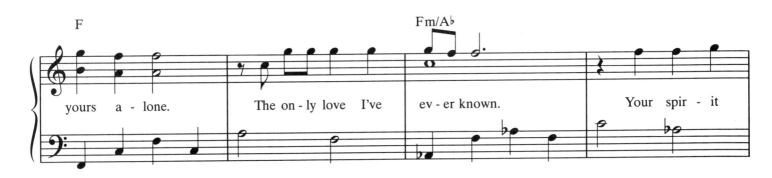

yours a - lone. The on - ly love I've ev - er known. Your spir - it

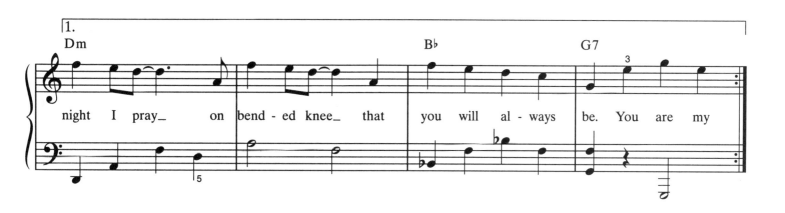

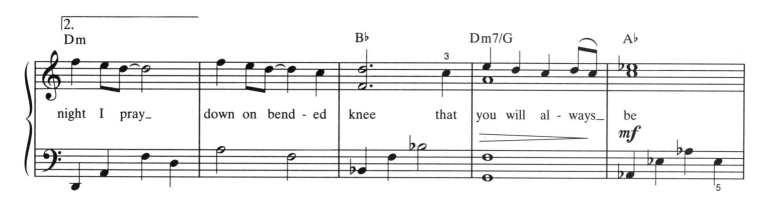

My Everything - 4 - 4

SHAPE OF MY HEART

Words and Music by
MAX MARTIN, RAMI
and LISA MISKOVSKY
Arranged by DAN COATES

Shape of My Heart - 4 - 1

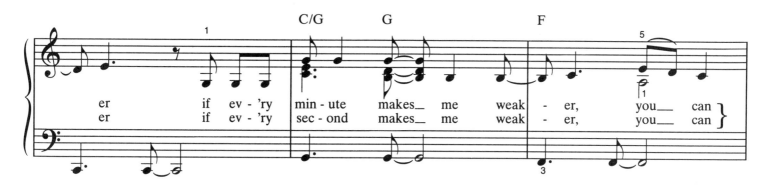

er   if ev - 'ry   min - ute   makes__ me   weak   - er,   you__ can
er   if ev - 'ry   sec - ond   makes__ me   weak   - er,   you__ can

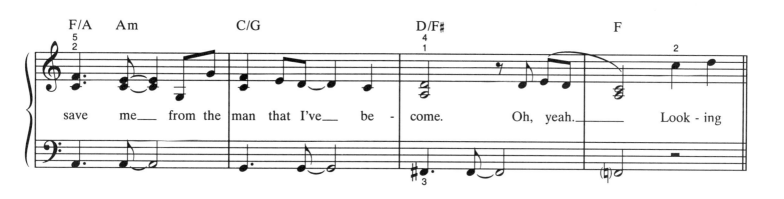

save   me__ from the   man that I've__ be - come.   Oh, yeah.___   Look - ing

Chorus:

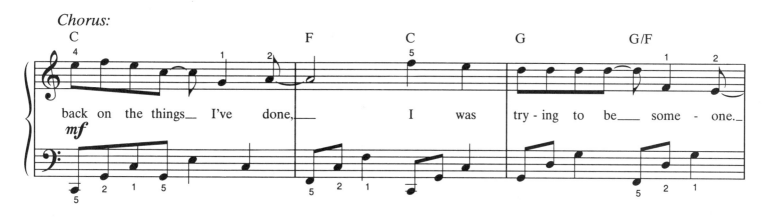

back on the things__ I've done,___   I   was   try - ing to be__ some - one.__

___   I played__ my part.___   and kept you in the   dark.   Now let me

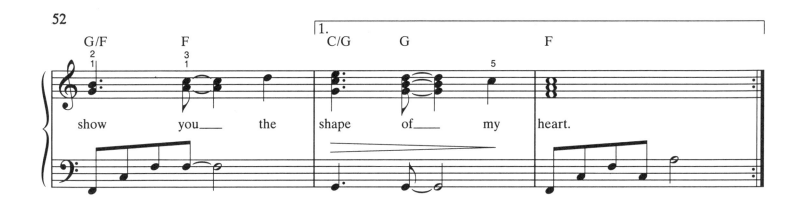

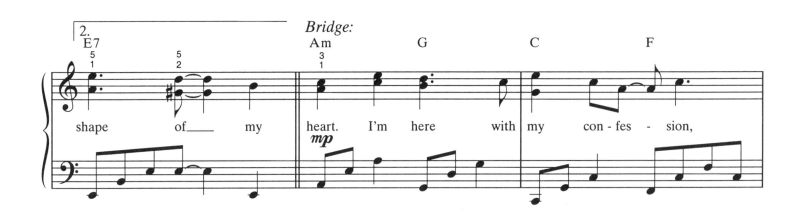

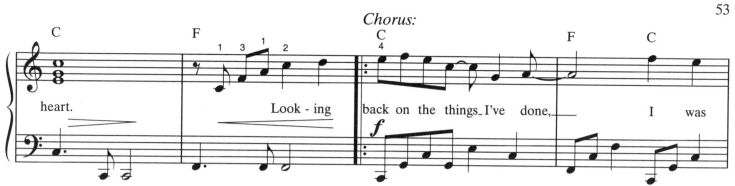

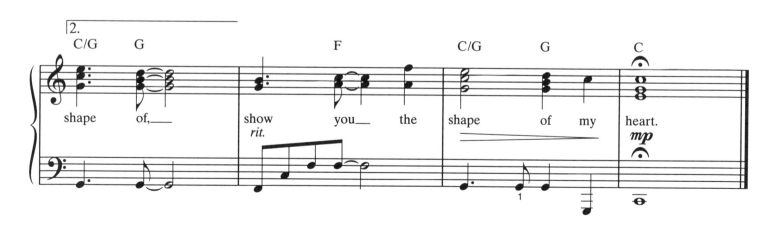

Shape of My Heart - 4 - 4

OOPS!...I DID IT AGAIN

Words and Music by
MAX MARTIN and **RAMI**
Arranged by DAN COATES

Moderate dance beat (♩ = 94)

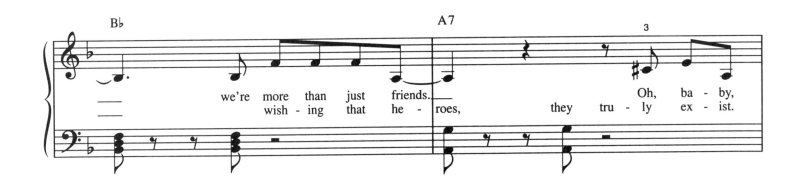

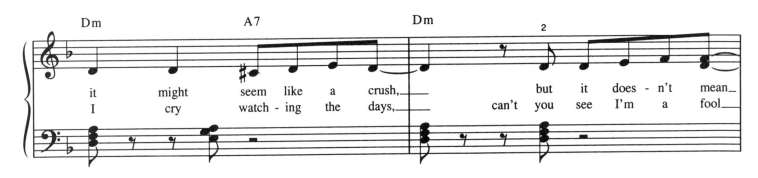

Oops!...I Did It Again - 5 - 1

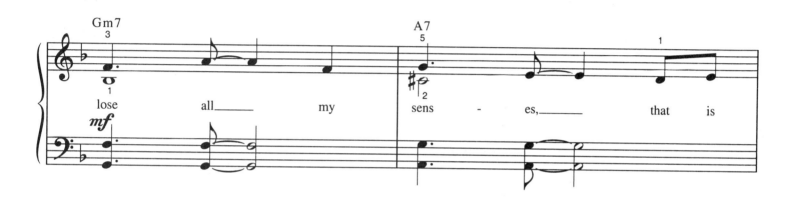

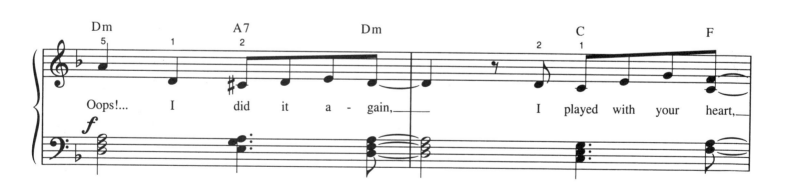

Oops...I Did It Again - 5 - 2

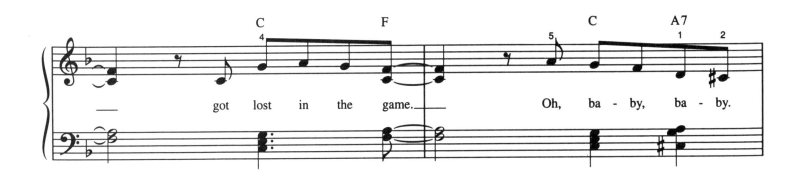

got lost in the game. ___ Oh, ba - by, ba - by.

Oops!... You think I'm in love, ___ that I'm sent from a - bove. ___

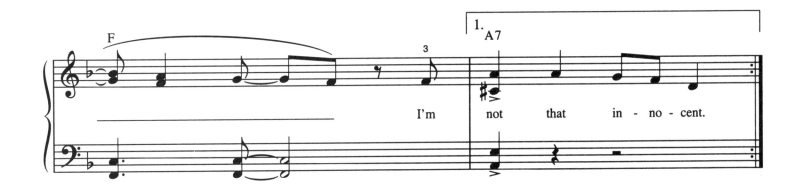

I'm not that in - no - cent.

2.

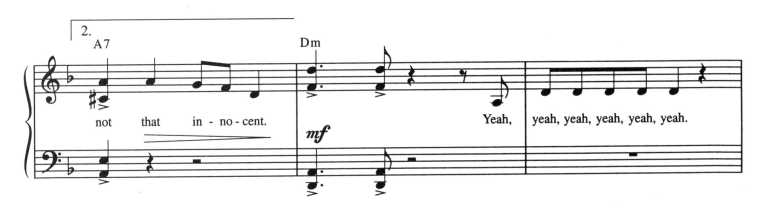

not that in - no - cent. *mf*   Yeah, yeah, yeah, yeah, yeah, yeah.

Yeah, yeah, yeah, yeah, yeah, yeah.

Oops!... I did it a - gain____ to your heart,____ got lost in this game, oh, ba - by.____

in this game, oh, ba - by.____ Oops!... You think that I'm sent____ from a - bove.____

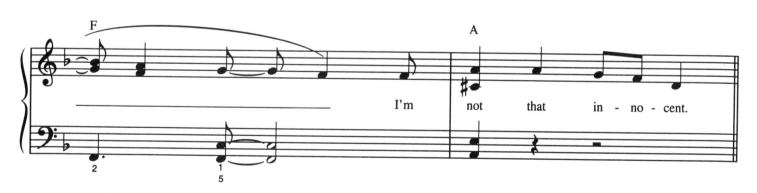

I'm not that in - no - cent.

58

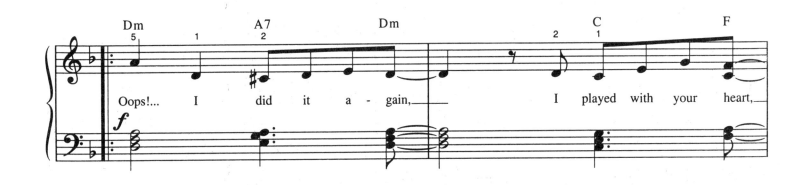

Oops!... I did it a - gain, I played with your heart,

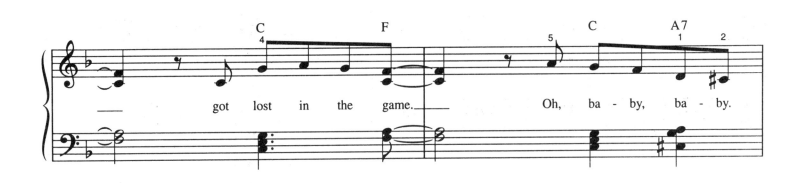

got lost in the game. Oh, ba - by, ba - by.

Oops!... You think I'm in love, that I'm sent from a - bove.

1.
I'm not that in - no - cent.

2.
not that in - no - cent.

SHOW ME THE MEANING
OF BEING LONELY

Words and Music by
MAX MARTIN and HERBERT CRICHLOW
Arranged by DAN COATES

Moderately slow

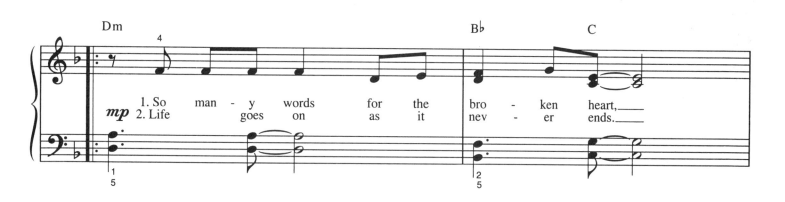

1. So man - y words for the bro - ken heart,____
2. Life goes on as it nev - er ends.____

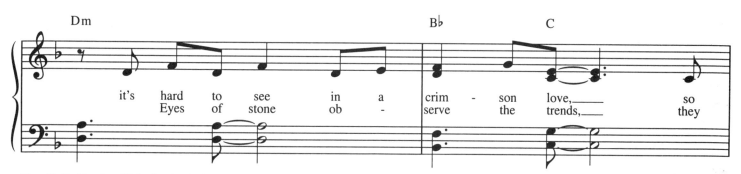

it's hard to see in a crim - son love,____ so
Eyes of stone ob - serve the trends,____ they

Show Me the Meaning of Being Lonely - 5 - 1

60

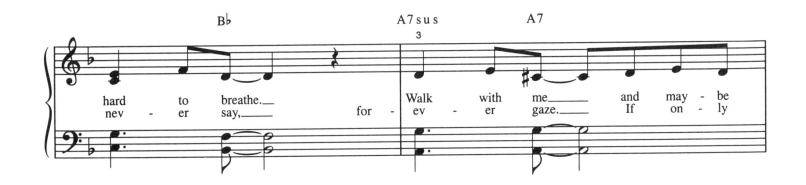

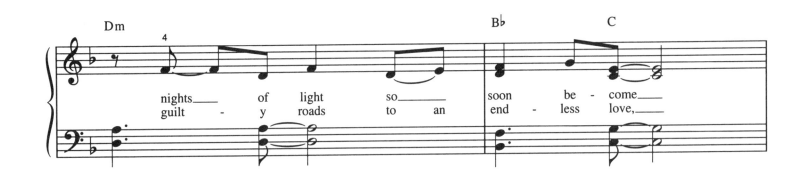

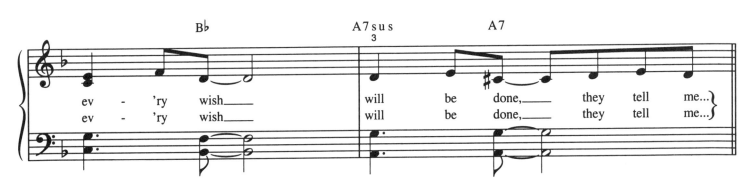

Show Me the Meaning of Being Lonely - 5 - 2

Show Me the Meaning of Being Lonely - 5 - 3

62

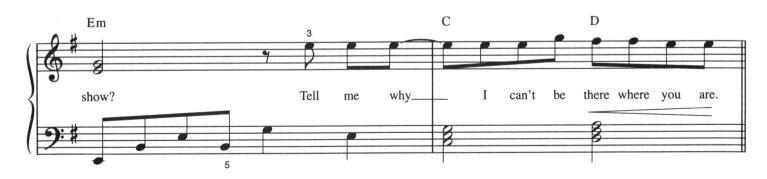

Show Me the Meaning of Being Lonely - 5 - 4

SOMETIMES

Words and Music by
JORGEN ELOFSSON
Arranged by DAN COATES

Moderately slow

Verse:

1.You tell me you're in love with me,
2. I don't wan - na be so shy.

like you can't take your pret - ty eyes a - way from me. ___
Ev - 'ry time that I'm a - lone I won - der why. ___

It's not that I don't
Hope that you will

want to stay,
wait for me,

but ev - 'ry time you
you'll see that

come too close, I move a - way. ___
you're the on - ly one for me. ___

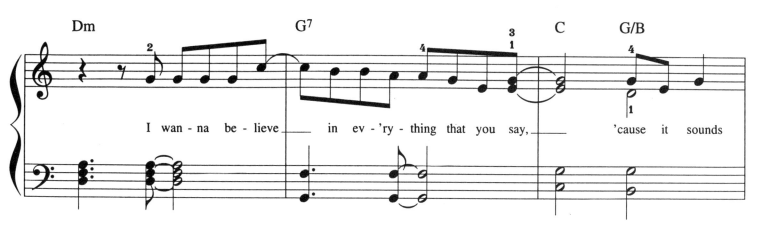

Sometimes - 4 - 2

To Coda ⊕

Sometimes - 4 - 4

STRONGER

Words and Music by
MAX MARTIN and RAMI
Arranged by DAN COATES

Moderately, with a strong beat (♩ = 108)

Stronger - 4 - 1

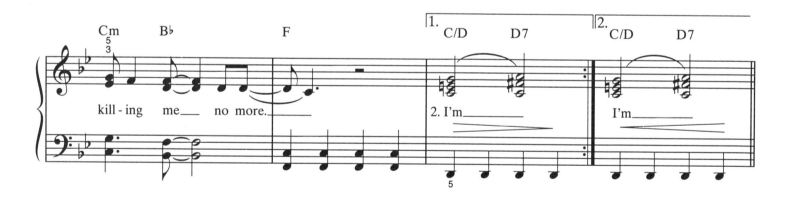

Stronger - 4 - 2

Oh, yeah.___ Here I go, on my own. I don't

need no-bod-y, bet-ter off a-lone. Here I go,___ on my own now.

I don't need no-bod-y, not an-y-bod-y.

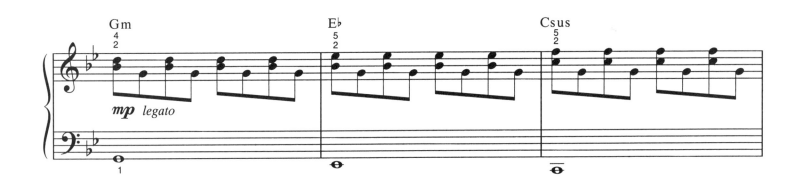

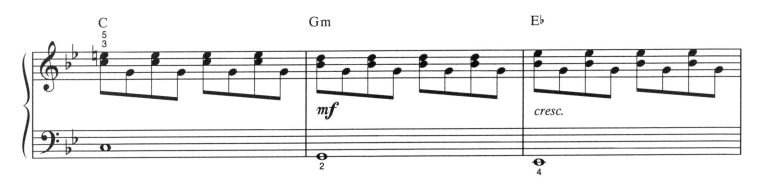

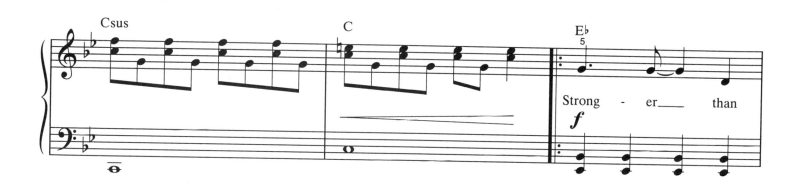

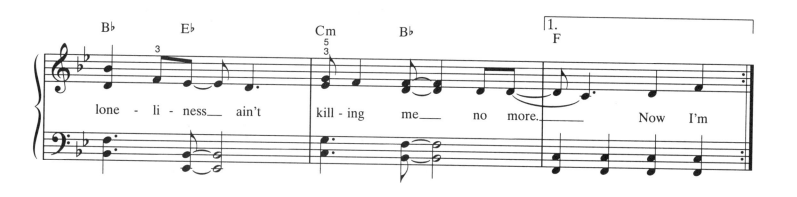

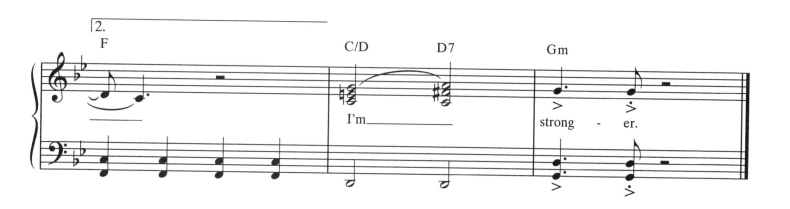

Stronger - 4 - 4

THAT'S THE WAY IT IS

Words and Music by
MAX MARTIN, KRISTIAN LUNDIN
and ANDREAS CARLSSON
Arranged by DAN COATES

74

THIS I PROMISE YOU

Words and Music by
RICHARD MARX
Arranged by DAN COATES

Slowly (♩ = 84)

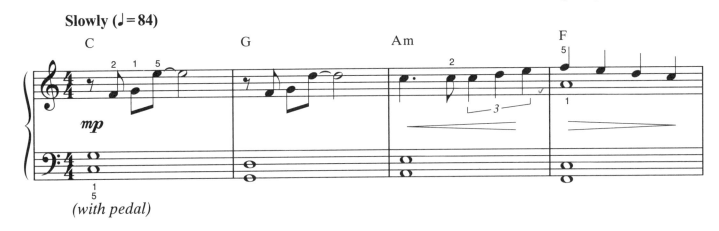

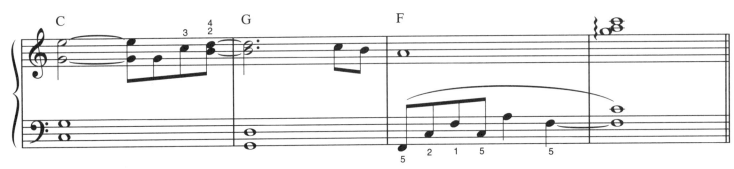

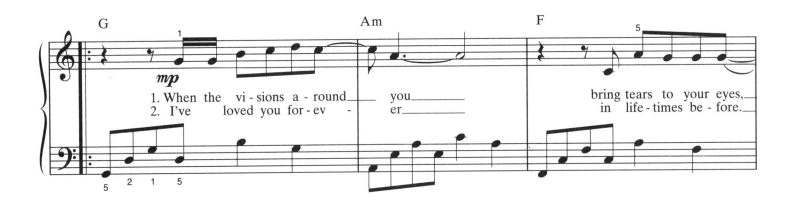

1. When the vi - sions a - round you bring tears to your eyes,
2. I've loved you for - ev - er in life - times be - fore.

and all that sur - rounds you
And I prom - ise you, nev - er

This I Promise You - 4 - 1

SOMEWHERE OUT THERE

Words and Music by
JAMES HORNER, BARRY MANN
and CYNTHIA WEIL
Arranged by DAN COATES

Moderately, with expression

TO LOVE YOU MORE

Words and Music by
JUNIOR MILES and DAVID FOSTER
Arranged by DAN COATES

To Love You More - 5 - 1

86

To Love You More - 5 - 4

A WHOLE NEW WORLD

Words by
TIM RICE

Music by
ALAN MENKEN
Arranged by DAN COATES

Moderately, with expression

90

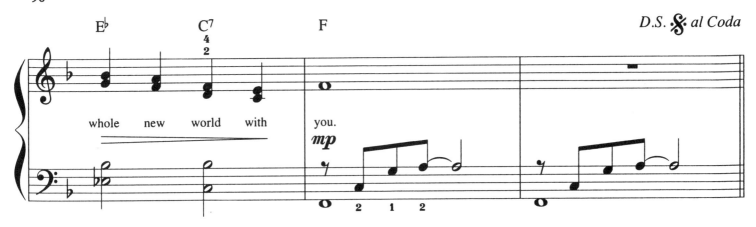

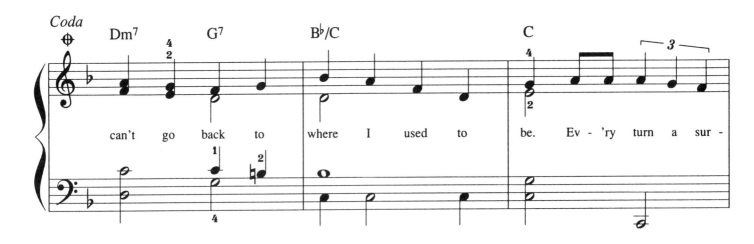

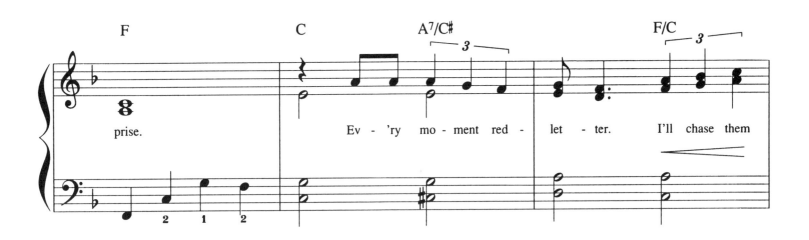

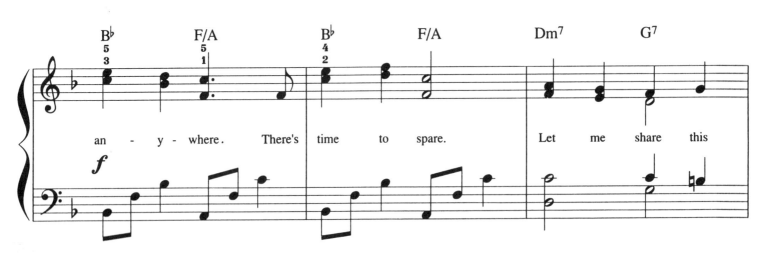

A Whole New World - 4 - 3